Critical Eye Contact: Learn How To Become More Authoritative, Dominant & Confidence With The Use Of Purposeful Eye Contact

Aiden Mccoy

© 2015

Disclaimer

Table of Contents

Introduction

Eye contact is perhaps our most effective non-verbal tool for connecting with others and communicating our thoughts and emotions. It is arguably the most revealing aspect of body language as a communication system. It indicates everything from confidence and respect to fear and nervousness, sometimes allowing us to communicate when speech is not possible, sometimes betraying thoughts and emotions we would rather not share.

Influenced by everything from religion to psychological health, the significance of eye contact and the customs surrounding it vary across cultures and from one individual to another. Its significance also changes depending the nature of the relationship between those who are using it. A parent-child relationship may use eye contact differently than a husband-wife relationship, and two friends would use it differently than would two enemies.

We use eye contact to wordlessly grant or deny permission, to gauge whether or not someone likes us, and to express agreement or disagreement. Because we tend to look at a person who is speaking, eye contact is often interpreted as a desire to initiate conversation. Conversely, we tend to avoid eye contact in order to maintain our privacy.

Eye contact is a versatile tool for establishing and breaking human connections, and it is the first method of communication we learn as human beings. In her 2014 *Forbes* article, "Fascinating Facts About Eye Contact," Carol Kinsey Goman, Ph.D., explains that the power of eye contact comes from its use as a survival tactic by early humans. In attracting and holding its mother's gaze, Goman explains, an infant increased its chances of receiving care. Eye contact between mothers and children retains its power in modern day society. Infants still instinctively make eye contact with their caregivers, and those connections still have profound effects on the parental mind. Eye contact is still a mother's most accurate means of assessing her child's intentions, emotions, and thought processes.

In a 2002 paper published by the National Academy of Sciences of the United States of America, Teresa Farroni, Gergely Csibra, Francesca Simiont, and Mark H. Johnson concluded that infants learn within their first year of life that the eye contact behaviors of others carry much significance, and a 2004 study published in the *Journal of Cognitive Neuroscience,* found that the direct gaze influences an infant's ability to recognize faces. In a 2001 paper published in the *International Journal of Behavioral Development,* authors Lohaus, Keller, and Voelker show a correlation between eye contact, infant crying, and maternal sensitivity. Their observations, conducted during the first 12 weeks of the infant's life, found that mothers who were more sensitive to their babies spent more time engaging them with direct eye contact, and that more eye contact equaled less crying.

In addition to facilitating our engagement with others as infants and throughout the courses of our lives, eye contact promotes learning by increasing our ability to retain and recall information. However, in a 2006 study outlined in the *British Journal of Developmental Psychology,* authors Phelps, Doherty-Sneddon, and Warnock, found that among five-year old children, those who broke eye contact while considering and formulating an answer to a question answered correctly more often than children who maintained eye contact. Because eye contact facilitates strong connections and reveals a lot of information, it demands the expenditure of significant amounts of processing power, hence it distracts the brain from other thought processes.

Perhaps because it is so mentally and emotionally demanding, some people—especially those who suffer from autism and social anxiety—find eye contact unsettling and even unbearable. In fact, eye contact is often used by psychology and psychiatry professionals as a tool for the evaluation of mental health. A patient's mental status is determined partially by the frequency with which she initiates and responds to eye contact, and whether or not she sustains or breaks it. The quality of her eye contact—its intensity or blankness—is also analyzed.

But an aversion to eye contact is not always rooted in an individual's mental health. Often, it is the result of cultural or religious conditioning. When it comes to the meaning and appropriateness of eye contact, western cultures differ greatly from eastern cultures. In Muslim cultures for example, women are taught to lower their gaze upon encountering a man, as it is considered inappropriate to gaze upon the features of the opposite sex. In Japan, the lowered gaze is read as a sign of respect for one's superiors, and school children are taught to look not at their instructor's face, but at his Adam's apple or the knot of his tie. Western culture on the other hand interprets a lack of eye contact as a sign of weakness. It is read as an indication of low self-confidence and it evokes suspicion regarding a person's intentions. On the other hand, even in western cultures, too much eye contact is considered invasive or threatening.

Eye contact can be used to improve friendships, romantic relationships, interactions with family, and business partnerships. It greatly influences how others feel about us, but in order to use it effectively and achieve the positive results we desire, we must closely monitor the quality of our eye contact in order to strike a very delicate balance between too much and too little, too intense and too shifty. This book will help you find that balance and teach you to use it to your advantage. You are about to learn just how big of an impact eye contact has on your life. This book will show you why eye contact is so uncomfortable and how to alleviate that discomfort, and it will outline tips and techniques for using eye contact in personal and business situations in order to make good impressions, establish trusting relationships, and persuade others to help you get what you want out of life.

Chapter 1: Why is Eye Contact Important?

According to Adrian Furnham, Ph.D., professor of psychology at University College London, the subject of eye contact, up until the mid-1960s, was considered a trivial waste of time. Today's culture on the other hand, could not attribute more significance to the human gaze if it tried. We deem eyes to be the windows to our souls. They project our true thoughts and feelings and our very essences to the rest of the world. Eye contact is our most primitive, and to this day, our most effective means of communication.

Eye contact creates a powerful subconscious connection between two people, and it reveals, sometimes too fully, what is really going on in our hearts and minds. Sadness, embarrassment, shame, and depression cause us to look away from others, while, on the other hand, we spend more time engaging in direct eye contact with those whom we love, like, admire, and respect. We even define the nature of our relationships based on eye contact. The more there is, the more intimate the relationship. But according to Goman, the amount of eye contact also depends on whether that intimacy is voluntary or forced. For example, people tend to avoid eye contact in elevators, crowded buses, and other situations that put them in close physical proximity to strangers.

The line between too little and too much eye contact is a thin one. In a personal setting, too much can feel invasive, threatening, condescending, or insolent. In a business setting, it may be interpreted as an attempt to dominate, intimidate, or otherwise reduce the stature of the other in order to give yourself the upper hand. All of these effects, whether intentional or not, result in defensiveness on the part of the person or people enduring your gaze, and for most people, the need to defend oneself doesn't leave much space for affinity, trust, or a desire to interact with you again in the future.

Conversely, too little eye contact can ruin relationships for opposite reasons. In both personal and business scenarios, it can make you appear uncomfortable, in which case, the other person or people present will wonder what they are doing wrong, which will make them uncomfortable as well. It also gives the impression that you are searching your surroundings for answers, which makes you appear unprepared. Most importantly, in western culture, we place a lot of weight on eye contact when it comes to determining a person's truthfulness. A person may interpret your inability to meet their gaze as a sign that you are lying or that you don't really care about them or what they have to say.

Of course, the ideal amount of eye contact will vary from one situation to another. For example, a speech at a business meeting will not involve the same amount or style of eye contact as will flirting with a person you want to date. Nor will you use the same amount of eye contact in speaking with a Muslim woman as you would when speaking with an atheist man from New York City.

Interestingly, eye contact also varies between genders. Woman tend to appreciate face-to-face conversations while men are more comfortable conversing while standing side by side.

In returning to Goman's 2014 *Forbes* article, we find that, thankfully, there is a rule of thumb we can apply to most situations. In order to foster productivity by creating a comfortable atmosphere, we should use direct eye contact 30% to 60% of the time. Also, it should be used less while speaking and more while listening. In fact, Furnham tells us, in his 2014 article, "The Secrets of Eye Contact, Revealed," that people tend to seek feedback and invite others to speak by looking up at the close of a grammatical break or when we are *finished* talking, thus using eye contact as a synchronizing signal that gives the conversation a comfortable rhythm. We also maintain that rhythm by looking away when we need time to think, reflect, or smooth out awkward speech.

An understanding of when and how long to look at people will enable you to persuade and influence them When used properly, eye contact creates an atmosphere of trust and mutual affinity between two people or in a group by establishing a level of connection with which everyone is comfortable. In most cases, highly successful people owe their accomplishments to help from others to some degree, and it is trust and likability that motivate people to believe in and support the manifestation of their dreams. Every politician and every salesman knows that, in seeking eye contact with their potential voter or customer, they make themselves appear more believable and more genuine. Eye contact is important because it is essential to your success in every aspect of life.

The way you employ your gaze is especially important when it comes to beginning new relationships—especially romantic ones. To look at another person is to invite interaction, and the more frank your gaze, the clearer your statement of high regard for your person of interest. Likewise, the your subject can either accept or deny your invitation just by returning your gaze or averting their eyes. If intimacy is not your goal, you'll want to change your approach. When the conversation itself is more important than the relationship between yourself and the person you're talking to, short, intermittent looks will foster higher productivity than longer lasting gazes. Basically, we can even determine what *types* of relationships we start and maintain with others just by using eye contact in a more conscious, more precise manner.

The length of a gaze is not its only meaningful attribute. According to Furnham, even seemingly inconsequential things like the direction of the gaze, the wideness of the eyes, pupil dilation, and blink rate all convey enormous amounts of information. In his 2014 *Psychology Today* article, Furnham describes a study that illustrates the power of just one of the above qualities—the dilated pupil. In the experiment, people were shown two photographs of a woman and asked to choose the most attractive one. In one picture, the woman's pupils were artificially dilated to twice their normal size. Other than that, both photos were exactly the same. The majority of viewers found the photo with the dilated pupils more attractive, and the most intriguing part is, most of them couldn't say why. Strong emotions like sexual attraction cause the pupils to dilate, and without knowing it, human beings perceive and interpret this change *and* reciprocate it.

The range of situations in which human beings make, break, or adjust eye contact in order to persuade others or to facilitate likability is nearly infinite. Furnham points out that Catholic confessionals and psychiatric couches are arranged to reduce eye contact, and by extension, the amount of embarrassment or shame the confessor experiences. The hitchhiker and the Salvation Army Santa ringing his bell outside the shopping mall both increase eye contact in order to get attention and influence others to contribute to their causes. Eye contact can also communicate one's desire to either co-operate or compete.

A thorough understanding of how to use eye contact ensures that other people, no matter their gender, age, or cultural background, and no matter the situation, will feel comfortable around you, trust you, and probably even like you. How you look at people often has a greater impact than the words you actually say to them.

Chapter 2: Why is Eye Contact so Uncomfortable?

Eye contact is our oldest and most effective means of communication, and it is essential to our survival and to our success in life...but that doesn't make it any less awkward. The reason eye contact is so uncomfortable is because it dramatically increases self-awareness, which, in turn, leads to an increase in self-consciousness. People also feel more emotionally charged when someone is looking straight into their eyes than they do when someone is looking away.

For those with self-esteem issues, the combination of heightened emotion and heightened self-awareness can be painful. We begin to ask ourselves if the person with whom we're sharing eye contact sees us the way we see ourselves. Is he looking at my giant zit and wondering what kind of contagious infection I have? Does she notice my love handles? Does he think I'm fat?

When we make direct eye contact with someone, our inner critic kicks into high gear. At the same time, we become more sensitive to the other person's facial expressions, sometimes imagining looks of disgust, condescension, or superiority that aren't really there. Essentially, we begin to project our own negative feelings about ourselves onto the person we are talking to, and because of our heightened emotional state, we react more strongly to the judgments we think the other person may be making about us.

Eye contact also establishes a very strong connection between two people. When someone looks directly into your eyes for the first time, you may feel as though your relationship has made a sudden leap from casual to intimate. If you are unprepared for intimacy with that person, or if you have no desire to become intimate with them, this drastic transition feels very uncomfortable. It can feel as though the inner workings of each person's mind and soul have been put on display for an entire audience, which is watching with amusement as the two of you try desperately to relate and to find some sort of shared zone in which you can exist comfortably together. Basically, it feels like walking onto a stage naked and being able to read the thoughts of every audience member as they form opinions about your body.

Feelings of discomfort and even violation are particularly intense for introverts and those who are extremely empathetic by nature. Certain personality types are so sensitive and so perceptive that they don't need to look a person in the eyes in order to feel their energy and their emotions. So when they do, the intensity of the signals they receive can make them feel like they are being ambushed or buried alive in the other person's thoughts and feelings.

Also, too much eye contact can be interpreted as a threat, which makes it nearly unbearable for those suffering from social anxiety disorder (SAD). A stronger than average fear response is a symptom of SAD, and it can be activated by a direct or lengthy gaze from a stranger. Eye contact can also be particularly difficult for those with autism. Processing all of the different aspects of another person's gaze is rather complex. We must interpret light reflections, pupil dilation, blinking, bloodshot capillaries, and eye movement along with the intensity and duration of the gaze. At the same time, we must listen to and interpret spoken words and attempt to properly apply subtle, nuanced social and cultural rules in order to formulate a proper response. Doing all of these things at once requires the ability to multi-task, which is very difficult for those with autism. For this reason, eye contact can be overwhelming to the point of sensory overload.

Most of us go through life unaware of the true complexity of eye contact, and we still find it difficult and uncomfortable. Dissecting the inner workings of the process might at first make it seem even more confusing and overwhelming, but breaking it down into its various elements allows us to study each one more closely and find out how all the different aspects are connected. Knowing how eye contact works enables us to use it to our advantage. There are many effective approaches to making eye contact more comfortable, and they can be used in personal situations, business scenarios, and when socializing.

It is hard to admit our shortcomings, but in acknowledging your need to work on eye contact, you've taken the first step to improving your conversational and social skills. No matter how shy or self-conscious you are, you too can learn to use eye contact to form positive, productive relationships with others.

Chapter 3: How to Make Eye Contact Easier

For those of us who find eye contact overwhelming, intimidating, or overstimulating, plunging right into it may only increase discomfort for us and for the people we're engaging with. You don't have to become an expert overnight. In fact, a gradual approach to improving eye contact will solidify your understanding and lead to more effective application. Once you've learned to properly use eye contact, you will find that focusing on the other person *distracts* you from your insecurities and your self-conscious inner monologue rather than amplifying them.

First, it's important to point out that if you're reading this book, you're aware of the importance of eye contact and of the possibility that you may not be using it to its fullest potential. This awareness is the first and most important step toward understanding and getting better at using eye contact. Also, your awareness indicates that you may be making more eye contact than you think you are, but that your discomfort is making your efforts feel inadequate. Basically, you may be better at making eye contact than you think you are, and that's a great starting point.

Also, it will help you to keep in mind that, while eye contact plays a major role in our social success, modern society is beginning to come to a better understanding and a greater acceptance of different personality types. Most people know the basic definitions of the words *introvert* and *extrovert,* for instance. And research into social anxiety and autism has contributed to a general awareness of how much social needs and abilities can vary from person to person. This means that, even if you are socially awkward, the person you're talking to is likely to give you some personality leeway rather than simply writing you off as a weirdo.

Learning to make more eye contact is a bit like trying to improve your diet. Say you cut out the sweets, cheeseburgers, and pizza all at once and fill your refrigerator with vegetables. You might be able to maintain this new regimen for about a week, after which point, you'll give into a craving and slip back into your old habits. Experts tell us that the best approach to changing eating habits is to gradually add healthy foods to your diet and allow them to replace the not-so-healthy ones over time. It's the same with eye contact. You don't have to immediately go out to the most popular bar in town and aim an unrelenting stare at the first person you see. As a matter of fact, you can improve your eye contact skills without socializing at all.

Studies have shown that just looking at a picture of someone who is staring directly into the camera stimulates the same responses as face-to-face eye contact with an actual person. So to begin with, stay at home and do a Google image search for faces. When you find photos of people making direct eye contact, spend some time looking at them. Once you become comfortable with this approach, apply the same technique to the television. Watch the news and try looking into the anchor's eyes as she reads you the evening headlines. News anchors are deliberately neutral and relatively unemotional, so maintaining eye contact with one through the television won't provoke overly intense responses. Once you're comfortable with the news anchor, move on to talk shows. Guests on talk shows tend to use more dramatic facial expressions and convey more emotion, and in trying to look each one in they eye, you'll learn to shift your attention from one speaker to another.

In addition to practicing eye contact, practice good posture. When we're not making eye contact, we're often lost in our own thoughts. Our eyes are unfocused and our gaze is aimed downward, causing our posture to sag. Sitting up straight makes you feel more alert and attentive. This brings your eyes into focus and makes it physically easier to aim your gaze at the person you're talking to. Good posture gives your conversation partner the impression that you're interested in what they have to say. If you're not used to maintaining a posture of alertness and attentiveness, it may be tiring at first, so it's a good idea to practice sitting up straight while you're practicing making eye contact with news anchors and talk show guests.

Even when practicing eye contact with real people in face-to-face scenarios, you can work slowly up to a direct gaze instead of plunging into it all at once. Start by looking between their eyes or just above their eyebrows. They probably won't detect the difference. It's also not necessary to maintain eye contact throughout the entire conversation. In fact, researchers agree that making less eye contact while you're speaking and more while you're listening creates the ideal balance for a comfortable environment. So to begin with, practice making eye contact only when you are listening to the other person speak.

Eye contact is also easier when used for a shorter duration. When you start practicing in person, begin with conversations you know will not last very long. For example, next time you go through a drive-through, look the cashier in the eyes as he hands you your food. Or, next time you go to the grocery store, look the cashier in the eyes as she hands you your receipt. These conversations are also easier because they are extremely casual.

Interactions with your grocery store cashier are relatively infrequent, and they carry less significance, so there is less pressure on you to make a perfect impression.

Another low-pressure way to approach eye contact is to start by using it with friends and family. It is much less intimidating to look someone in the eyes if you are already comfortable with them. Once you become proficient at using eye contact with people you know, you will be able to move on to people like your attractive co-worker or your boss.

For some, taking a systematic approach to eye contact practice will be enormously helpful, while for others, it may add complexity and stress. If planning helps you, go for it. If it doesn't, just try making as much eye contact as you can in social situations. However, planning out your at home practice will benefit you either way. In fact, making an actual schedule for at home practice will add legitimacy and importance to your efforts. It will also hold you accountable, thus driving you to make more effort, which, as we all know, produces better results.

Chapter 4: The Relationship Between Eye Contact & Attraction

Researchers have found that women from cultures as different as Papua New Guinea and the United States use the same eye contact-based flirting tactic—the one where the woman holds a man's gaze for a long moment then tilts her head down and away while smiling. Because this tactic is so ubiquitous across cultures and time, German ethologist Irenaus Eibl-Eibesfeldt believed the behavior to be innate. This means that eye contact, in addition to being our oldest and most effective means of communication and survival, is also our oldest and most effective means of initiating romantic relationships.

In western cultures, both men and women show their attraction to one another by gazing at their person of interest for two or three seconds, then lowering their eyelids and looking away. Helen E. Fisher tells us in her

1993 *Psychology Today* article, "The Biology of Attraction," that eye contact triggers a primitive section of the brain which responds with one of two recommended courses of action—approach or retreat. Thus when we discover that another person has locked their gaze on us, we find it impossible not to respond. While we're deciding whether to stay and flirt or refuse the invitation and flee, we use *displacement gestures* to alleviate the anxiety of being put on the spot. These gestures are just meaningless stalling tactics, like adjusting your clothes and hair or rifling through your wallet or purse for nothing in particular.

Eye contact elicits immediate responses, one of which—dilated pupils—is a sign of intense attraction. If your subject of interest chooses to stay and talk, pay close attention to their pupils during the conversation. According to Psychologist Eckhard Hess, our pupils dilate to take in more light when we're looking at a person or thing that interests us, and they contract when our gaze falls on something less intriguing. This concept extends to conversation in that, when we are interested in the topic at hand, our pupils dilate, and when we get bored with it, they contract. Once you've attracted someone's attention, good conversation is essential to keeping it. Paying attention to pupil activity enables you to adjust the topic of conversation in order to keep the other person interested and heighten attraction.

Don't study your love interest's pupils too closely though. Unrelenting eye contact is often interpreted as a threat or an attempt at domination, both of which will obviously make your date feel vulnerable and overly studied. This can lead to self-consciousness and cause the other person to shut down and block your advances.

If you just met the man or woman with whom you're speaking, try making eye contact about 50 percent of the time. Make sure you look at them when *they* are speaking. This gives the impression that you are interested in what they have to say. On the other hand, it is better to look away when *you* are talking. This allows the other person to listen to you without feeling attacked or pressured. It gives them space and time in which to process what you are saying and formulate a response. Also, studies have found that it is easier to think clearly when *not* looking into the eyes of another, as the intense emotion triggered by eye contact can be incredibly distracting. Hence looking away while you're speaking increases the chances that you will say something intelligent or clever.

The direction in which the man or woman is gazing when they are speaking indicates both attraction and intention. According to psychologists, a person looks to their left while reminiscing or trying to recall facts or memories. If the person speaking is sharing true stories from his or her past, they probably feel comfortable with you, which is a sign of attraction. Likewise, the effort to recall facts correctly indicates that the person wants to impress you with their knowledge of the subject at hand. Conversely, if the man or woman looks to the right while speaking, he or she is accessing the creative half of their brain, which, among other things, is a tool for weaving fiction. This may indicate that the attraction conveyed by their other non-verbal signals is a guise intended to distract you from their real intentions. Looking to the right is also a universal sign of boredom.

Increased blinking is also a good indication of attraction since our blinking rate tends to increase when we like someone. Winking, is another eye gesture we use to convey interest, but while it can be effective when done right, it can also come off as a little creepy when used improperly. For instance, it should not be used from across a crowded bar to initiate first contact with a woman you've never seen before. Winking carries connotations of a shared secret, so it can be interpreted as rather forward. It's more effective and more appropriate when used with someone you've been successfully flirting with for at least a few hours. Say your best friend steals you away and walks you across the bar to meet his brother. Looking back over your shoulder and winking at the woman you've been flirting with lets her know that you're still interested and that you'll come find her again when you have the chance.

In this context, the wink has more playful connotations, which for most people is more attractive than forwardness.

Overall, eye contact is a reliable indicator of romantic attraction. Use it to initiate contact, and if your man or woman of interest chooses to stay and talk, use it to gauge their interest and adjust the topic of conversation to maintain intrigue. Look them in the eye while they are speaking, and look away while you are speaking. Pay attention to their pupils, their blink rate, and the direction of their gaze when they are looking away. This may seem like a lot to think about, and indeed, trying to interpret all these signals on the spot, when you're probably already a little nervous, may confuse and overwhelm you. Just remember, eye contact is our oldest and most effective tool for communication. You have an innate understanding of how to use it. If eye contact makes you uncomfortable, try practicing with some of the techniques in the previous chapter before using it in flirting situations. Otherwise, just try to relax and trust your instincts. They will lead you in the right direction.

Chapter 5: Tips & Techniques

Even though eye contact is an innate tool for communication and relationship-building, most of us would still like to know how to wield it more effectively. Even the most confident and outgoing among us can benefit from taking the time to refine their approach to eye contact. After all, if you're going to use one of the most powerful tools in the human arsenal, you may as well use it to its fullest potential. The following techniques can be used to initiate and improve relationships of all kinds, and to foster productivity during all types of meetings and discussions. They will enhance everything from your parenting abilities to your success in business.

First, let's take a look at the masters of eye contact—the salesmen, politicians, and motivational speakers who make their living by gaining the attention, trust, and support of others. All of them, from the presidential candidates to the street performers, know that an understanding of eye contact is crucial to their success. We've all walked down a bustling downtown street on a Saturday night and seen the guy on the corner singing his heart out over the rhythms of his beat-up guitar. Think about how you feel as you approach the open guitar case lying on the sidewalk half full of loose change and one-dollar bills. Do you want to cross the street in order to avoid the performer, or do want to stand and watch him for a minute and then throw in your pocket change?

Maybe you never noticed before, but you choose your course of action in this situation the same way you choose your course of action when you notice a stranger trying to flirt with you—you decide based on eye contact. If the street musician engages you with direct eye contact and smiles as you approach, his performance will seem more personalized and more energetic, and you will be more likely to tip him. On the other hand, if he looks down or off to the side, he'll create an uncomfortable disconnect that will make stopping to throw your dollar into that guitar case feel awkward and uncomfortable. Next time you see a street performer, look at his tip container, then look at his eyes. If the container is nearly empty, chances are he won't be returning your gaze.

Eye contact is what sells you, your ideas, and your product, whether you are playing music on a busy downtown corner, soliciting votes during a presidential campaign, or asking the head of your company to fund your next innovative project. However, you will need to adjust your use of eye contact depending on your situation and on how many people you're talking to.

When speaking to a group, maintain eye contact with your whole audience, not just one person. In focusing on one individual throughout your speech, you lose the interest of the others. Instead, switch your focus to a different person each time you begin a new sentence. This keeps your whole audience interested.

When speaking to one person, whether a love interest, a friend, or a colleague, use direct eye contact mostly while they are speaking. Break your gaze every few seconds or so, looking up and to one side, preferably the left. This will tell your conversation partner that you are trying to remember something, which will make them feel that you are trying to add to the conversation and keep it going. Whatever you do, don't look down. This indicates an end to the conversation.

If your situation requires you to do most of the listening—say if you are a therapist or counselor—be careful not to use too much direct eye contact, as this can make an already uncomfortable person feel even more vulnerable. Steven Atchison, an author on personal development, recommends a method he calls *the triangle,* in which you look at one eye for a few seconds, look at the other eye for a few seconds, then shift your gaze to the mouth for a few seconds, continuing the rotation as the person speaks. Atchison also recommends nodding and using words of agreement to show interest and keep the speaker talking.

Eye contact can also help you win an argument without saying a single word. During an argument, direct eye contact makes your opponent feel smaller and weaker. It surprises and confuses them, distracting them from their point. Holding your opponent's gaze during an argument, both while they are speaking and while you are speaking, shows strength and confidence. If someone is deliberately trying to provoke you, remain silent and stare straight at them. Just don't look away. If you do, you immediately loose the argument.

If you want to show another person that you like them, use your eyes to explore their whole face. Listen to what they are saying and react with facial gestures such as raised eyebrows or a smile. At the same time, shift your gaze between their eyes, their nose, their cheeks, and their mouth. By taking in every part of the person's face, you maintain eye contact without overwhelming them with a constant, fixed gaze. You also show that you are interested in many of their various features, which translates to being interested in the many aspects of their personality and their life. You make it plain that you want to know more about them without coming off like a desperate, creepy stalker.

When you want to convey that you more-than-like someone, share a prolonged gaze with them. Extended eye contact is perhaps the most universal non-verbal way to say *I love you*—especially when there is no speaking involved. The ability to comfortably share silent, direct eye contact conveys and increases feelings of love, intensifying the connection between two people to the point that they feel as though they *are* having a very meaningful conversation—one that only they understand.

Using the above techniques will help you cultivate the kinds of trusting, supportive relationships that the most successful individuals in the world depend on to manifest their dreams. Whether you are shy or self-confident, these approaches will help to refine your approach to eye contact and make it your most effective tool for establishing productive personal connections.

Chapter 6: Common Eye Contact Mistakes

Most of us realize just how essential eye contact is when it comes to making a positive, lasting first impression, but our hyper-awareness of its importance doesn't make us feel more comfortable with it. In fact, it makes most of us even more nervous, which leads to increased awkwardness. There are a few common eye contact mistakes that everyone should look out for—including those who feel perfectly comfortable initiating new relationships.

The most common mistake a person can make with eye contact is to approach the use of it under the assumption that everyone you meet is like you. Most of us like to think that we're aware of diversity, that we accept and even appreciate it, but most of us also surround ourselves daily with people who live lives and cherish values that are similar to our own. We take for granted that everyone around us thinks and acts the way we do.

We need to keep in mind that the world is filled with a multitude of cultures and personality types, and that because modern life is powered by a global economy, we are bound to run into someone whose lifestyle, personality, and values run contrary to our own. When using eye contact, do not assume that, because you take it as a sign of respect, and because you are perfectly comfortable with it, the person you're speaking to must feel the same way. Instead, try to read the other person. As you come to know more about them, adjust your use of eye contact accordingly.

Hyper-awareness is the primary culprit in our second most common eye contact mistake. We try so hard to show that we understand the value of eye contact that we overuse it. We go to job interviews and stare our hiring managers right in the eyes throughout the conversation. We go on first dates and stare straight into our love interest's eyes from appetizer through dessert. Too much eye contact, no matter what the situation, is just as awkward, if not more so, than too little. While too little gives the impression that you lack self-confidence or that you lack interest in a conversation, too much is creepy, intimidating, and uncomfortably forward. Balance is key to using eye contact to its fullest potential. Practicing some of the techniques mentioned in previous chapters will help you achieve that balance.

Our desire to project self-confidence is the underlying cause of our third most common eye contact blunder. We all understand that in situations where we must take the lead or give a speech, eye contact will convince our followers or our audience that we are a trusted authority on the subject at hand. But staring at our audience the entire time we are talking does not convince them that we are knowledgeable, it makes them feel attacked. Maintaining an unrelenting gaze while you are talking is a good approach when you want to win an argument against an equally determined opponent, but when you need your audience to feel comfortable in your presence, attack mode will only achieve the opposite. Your audience will wonder why you are being so forceful in your attempts to convince them, and they will become suspicious of your motives and your truthfulness.

Truthfulness—or a lack of it—is the driving force behind another common eye contact blunder. In western culture, eye contact represents honesty, therefore, when we suspect someone is lying, we interpret a shifty gaze as proof that we are right. In many cases, the dishonest person knows this and will overuse eye contact in an attempt to alleviate suspicion. This means that, in most cases, more eye contact does not necessarily equal more honesty.

Likewise, less eye contact does not necessarily equal dishonesty. As mentioned before, different personalities use eye contact in different ways. If we are going to assume that everyone who fails to make eye contact is lying, we may as well automatically label every shy, introverted, or socially anxious person a liar. That may sound absurd and extreme, but it illustrates the need to be careful when interpreting the eye contact habits of others.

You may have noticed that all of our most common eye contact mistakes take root in a shared theme. They all result from our tendency to misinterpret those who are different from us. They are caused by our desire to create efficiency by making assumptions about others based on what we know of ourselves, our cultures, our personalities, and our lifestyles. If we are going take full advantage of the power of eye contact and use it to benefit ourselves and others, we must do so with patience. We must take the time to combine what we know of the person or people in question with what we know of the situation at hand in order to formulate the best approach to using and interpreting eye contact in every unique set of circumstances. Aside from an understanding of eye contact itself, patience is our most effective tool for forming and maintaining positive, productive relationships.

Conclusion

Since mankind's most primitive days, eye contact has been our best means of forming relationships in order to ensure our own survival. We use it to convey thoughts, emotions, needs, and desires. We use it to engender trust and gain support. It is the clearest and most revealing form of non-verbal communication we have at our disposal, and in understanding how best to use and interpret it, we gain the ability to cultivate productive family and work relationships that will assist us in manifesting our grandest dreams.

Eye contact creates powerful connections between human beings, and the way two people use it varies depending on the nature of their relationship. The ways in which we engage in or avoid eye contact reveals the intensity of our attraction or opposition to others and defines the amount of intimacy in a relationship. We can use it to either start conversations or avoid them.

An understanding of the effects of too much or too little eye contact is essential to our ability to form positive relationships. No matter what the situation, too much eye contact elicits feelings of suspicion or defensiveness in the person we're talking to, while too little projects a lack of self-confidence. Finding the right balance of eye contact allows us to communicate productively in any type of situation.

It is likely that, at some point, each of us will find ourselves in a situation where we need to influence or persuade another person or a group of people in order to accomplish our goals or get what we want. In order to convince others to believe in us and work with us, we need to get them to trust us and like us. Knowing when and for how long to look a single individual or an entire audience in the eye is essential to inspiring trust and likability.

Eye contact makes all off us uncomfortable to some degree. This is because it creates intense self-awareness and self-consciousness and heightens emotions. The strength of a connection created through first eye contact can also be rather jarring since it suddenly and drastically increases the level of intimacy in the relationship. This intimacy can be extraordinarily uncomfortable for introverts and those with social anxiety or autism. In taking the time to break down the various elements of eye contact, you increase your understanding of how to use and interpret it, and your new-found understanding will dramatically increase your comfort level.

Remember, you don't have to become an eye contact expert overnight. A gradual approach to integrating eye contact will produce better results in the end. You can even practice at home using photographs, reality shows, and talk shows before you try using eye contact in real social situations. When you start using eye contact in person, work gradually up to the direct gaze by looking at the person's other facial features, and by only making eye contact while listening to the other person speak. It will also help you to begin by using eye contact only with people you already know and like, and with extremely casual acquaintances as these types of relationships put less pressure on you.

Once you become accustomed to using eye contact in more casual social situations, you can try using it to initiate romantic relationships. A thorough understanding of eye contact will enable you to trigger the approach response in your man or woman of interest rather than the retreat response. Remember, pupil dilation indicates sexual attraction and interest in the topic of conversation. In paying attention to it, you can adjust the conversation to maintain or increase the other person's interest, and, by extension, their attraction to you. Remember also to make eye contact mainly while the other person is speaking in order to assure him or her that you are interested. Most importantly, don't try too hard to manipulate the situation with eye contact. Just relax and trust your instincts.

Always keep in mind that eye contact is what sells you, your ideas, and your product. In refining your use of this powerful tool of persuasion, remember to adjust your methods according to the number of people you're talking to, your relationship to them, and the environment in which you're speaking to them. This will allow you to convey that you like, love, or want to collaborate with someone, or it can help you win an argument against even the most formidable opponent.

Remember to avoid making the assumption that everyone reads and interprets eye contact the same way you do. Take the time to get to know a person, and as you find out more about them, adjust your approach to account for different personalities and different religious and cultural backgrounds. Also, try not to let a hyper-awareness of the various elements of eye contact overwhelm you and make you even more uncomfortable. As a human being, you have an innate understanding of how to use it. The techniques and insights in this book are meant only to enhance and call forth that understanding so that you can apply it to your everyday life.

Eye contact may be our oldest and most primitive means of communication, but even in today's rapidly-evolving world of advanced technology, it remains our most powerful tool for forming relationships and exercising influence. Even with our incredible understanding of psychology, there is no better way to get inside the hearts and minds of other people than to look them straight in the eyes. Eye contact enables us to convey our thoughts and feelings and interpret those of others with a precision that not even the most eloquent string of spoken or written words could achieve. For this reason, an understanding of how to use eye contact is absolutely essential to our ability to initiate and cultivate positive relationships of all types. In making the effort to master the use of eye contact, you have improved your chances of gaining the trust and support of others, and of achieving your grandest goals.